STARTING RIDING

Helen Edom
and Lesley Sims

Designed by Joe Pedley
Illustrated by Norman Young
Photographs by Kit Houghton
Consultant: Jane Pidcock B.H.S.A.I.
Studio Photograph: Howard Allman

Contents

SCHOLASTIC INC.
New York Toronto London Auckland Sydney

First things

This book shows you how to ride a pony safely while it is walking, trotting, cantering and even jumping. You can learn how to make the pony understand what you want it to do. Later in this book, you can also find out how to care for a pony.

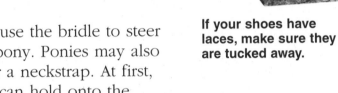

This is a back protector. You wear it for jumping.

What to wear

You should dress in comfortable clothing and wear sturdy shoes or boots. You also need a riding hat to stop you from hurting your head if you fall. Most riding schools can lend you a hat for your first lessons.

A riding hat has a strap to keep it on firmly.

Riding gloves stop your hands from getting rubbed.

Saddles and bridles

A pony wears a saddle and a bridle to make it easier for you to ride. The saddle is like a leather seat on its back. The bridle is buckled around the pony's head.

You use the bridle to steer the pony. Ponies may also wear a neckstrap. At first, you can hold onto the neckstrap to help you keep your balance.

If your shoes have laces, make sure they are tucked away.

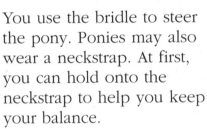

Being safe

Always walk around the front of ponies, not behind them. This is because ponies may kick with their back legs if they are startled.

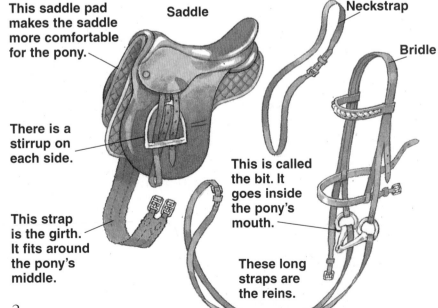

This saddle pad makes the saddle more comfortable for the pony.

Saddle

Neckstrap

Bridle

There is a stirrup on each side.

This strap is the girth. It fits around the pony's middle.

This is called the bit. It goes inside the pony's mouth.

These long straps are the reins.

Different colors

Ponies come in all kinds of different colors. Each type has its own name. Here are some to look out for.

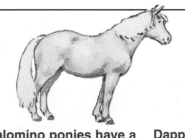  

Palomino ponies have a gold body and a white tail and mane.

Dapple-gray ponies are white with silver markings on them.

Piebald ponies have black and white patches all over them.

Going up to a pony

A helper will hold the pony for you.

A pony's shoulders are just in front of its saddle.

Ponies in a riding school are used to lots of different riders.

Before you go up to a pony, find out its name if you can. Say the name quietly and walk up to the pony's shoulder. Move steadily so you do not surprise or frighten the pony. Stroke the pony on its neck. Most ponies also enjoy a gentle scratch on their mane.

Stand beside the pony so you do not get stepped on if it moves.

3

How to get on

Getting on a pony is called mounting. At first, it is easier if someone helps you up. Later, you can learn to mount the pony by yourself.

A helper holds the pony's head. Without a helper, the pony may walk forward as you are trying to mount.

Before you mount

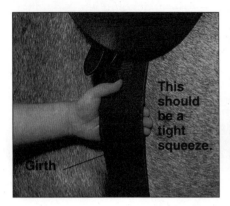

This should be a tight squeeze.

Girth

Stirrup

The loops are called stirrup leathers.

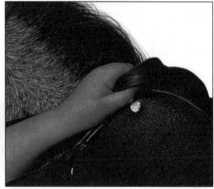

1. Slide your fingers under the girth. If it's loose, ask for help to tighten it so it holds the saddle firmly in place.

2. Get the stirrups ready. Take hold of each stirrup and slide it down to the bottom of the leather loop.

3. Pick up the reins and hold them in your left hand, like this. It helps if you also grasp some mane.

Taking a leg up

1. Holding the reins in your left hand, face the pony's left shoulder. Rest your left hand on the pony's neck and put your right hand on the front of the saddle.

2. Bend your left knee so that the helper can hold your leg. He will count to three, then push you up. Don't worry about pulling on your pony's mane.

3. Swing your right leg over the pony's back so that you land gently in the saddle. Remember to move your right hand off the saddle as you sit down.

Mounting by yourself

1. Stand beside the pony's left shoulder facing its tail. Hold the reins as before, throwing the ends over the pony's neck so that they are out of the way.

2. Turn the stirrup toward you with your right hand and place your left foot inside it. Rest your left hand on the pony's neck as you did when taking a leg up.

3. Put your right hand on the front of the saddle. Still holding the reins in your left hand, hop around on your right leg until you are facing the saddle.

Tall ponies

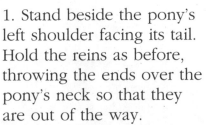

4. Now push off your right leg, to pull yourself up. Stand on the stirrup with your left foot. Use the front of the saddle to help pull yourself up.

5. Swing your right leg over the saddle, moving your right hand out of the way as before. Try to sit down gently so that you do not hurt the pony's back.

It is easier to reach the stirrup on a tall pony if you stand on a strong box when you mount. Some riding stables use milk crates or hay bales.

Sitting on a pony

When you begin to ride, a helper will lead your pony. This helps you to learn to sit safely without worrying about steering.

Reins

While you are learning, knot the reins to keep them out of the way.

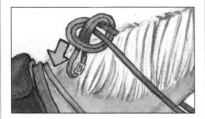

Stirrups

To put your feet into the stirrups, lift your knees and turn in your toes.

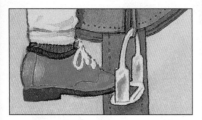

Try to push in your toes without looking down.

The widest part of your foot rests on the stirrup.

Sitting comfortably

To sit comfortably on your pony, sit in the middle of the saddle. Let your legs hang loosely so their weight rests in the stirrups.

Bend your elbows so your hands are just above your pony's neck. Try riding like this, before you pick up the reins.

Sit up, so your head, hips and heels are all in a straight line.

If you feel wobbly, hold onto the neckstrap or the saddle.

Your heels should be slightly lower than your toes.

The helper holds the pony with a strap called a leading rein.

Moving the stirrups

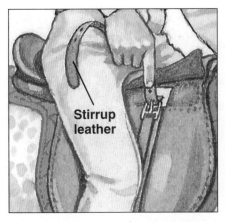

1. If your stirrups feel too long or too short, hold the end of the stirrup leather, pull it up and free the buckle with your finger.

2. Slide the leather up or down until the stirrup feels comfortable. Try to do this with one hand, keeping your foot in the stirrup.

3. Fasten the buckle into the nearest hole and tuck the end of the leather under your leg. Make sure it is flat or it will rub your leg.

Test your balance

Try these balancing exercises while someone holds your pony.

Your instructor may call out parts of the pony for you to touch.

Try to keep your legs still as you turn.

With both hands, touch your knees, then reach down to touch your toes. Sit up to touch the back of the saddle.

Using one hand at a time, stroke the pony's neck. See how close you can reach toward the pony's head. Try going farther each time.

Stretch out your arms and turn so that one hand points at the pony's ears and the other at his tail. Then try it the other way.

First steps

When the pony walks, it moves one leg at a time.
You can feel a slight bump as each leg moves.

You don't need the reins if someone leads you.

You should feel comfortable, not stiff.

Sit quietly, making yourself as tall you can. This helps both you and the pony to feel comfortable.

If you move around or lean forward, like the rider above, the pony will find you awkward to carry.

Try to keep your balance even when the pony stops or starts. Hold the neckstrap whenever you feel unsteady.

Improving your balance

When you feel ready, there are more exercises to help to improve your balance. Ask if you may try these while your pony is walking along.

Hold your arms out in front of you and swing them around in circles going over your shoulders.

Touch your head and your knees, then touch your hands together behind your back.

Holding the reins

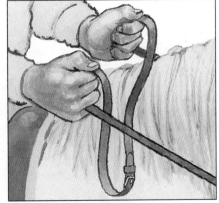

You should be able to just feel the pony's mouth.

When you can keep your balance really well, you can learn to hold the reins. Unknot them and pick up each side with your thumb on top like this.

Then move your little finger beneath the reins. Keep your hands gently closed so that you do not grip too tightly. Make sure your hands are level.

Always remember that the reins go to a metal bit which rests inside the pony's mouth. You can hurt the pony if you tug at the reins.

Practicing at home

Line up two chairs, one in front of the other. Tie a long piece of string to either side of the chair in front. Don't pull too hard on the string or the chair will fall over.

See how quickly you can get your fingers in the right place.

Riding in a ring

It is safest to start riding in a fenced-off area called a ring or arena. Your teacher, or riding instructor, stands in the middle and tells you what to do. Sometimes the instructor controls your pony on a long line called a longe line.

On the longe line, your pony moves in circles around the instructor.

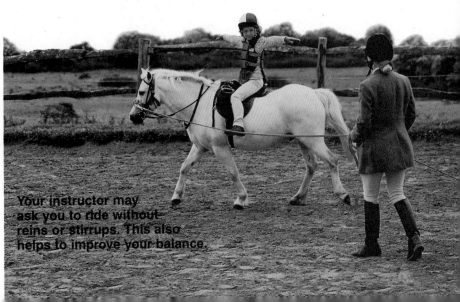

Your instructor may ask you to ride without reins or stirrups. This also helps to improve your balance.

Going wherever you want

You can give signals to your pony with your voice, legs and hands. These tell the pony what you want it to do. When you can give clear signals, you can ride by yourself.

Asking your pony to start

Squeeze like this.

When you squeeze your pony, try to keep the rest of your body still.

Squeeze the pony's side with both heels when you want it to start or walk faster. It helps to say "walk" firmly.

Try not to pull back on the reins as the pony starts to move. Say "good pony" as soon as the pony obeys.

Shortening reins

If your reins are too long, the pony won't feel your commands through its mouth. Use the thumb and first finger of one hand to pull the rein up through the other hand.

This hand stays still.

This hand pulls.

The rein slides through.

Asking your pony to stop

Never pull for very long.

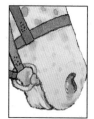

The reins make the bit press on the pony's mouth.

Sit up tall and close your legs briefly on the pony's sides. Move your hands back to tighten the reins.

Loosen the reins and then try again and again until the pony stops. It also helps to say "ha-aalt" calmly.

This rider is practicing stopping and turning.

Turning the pony

Turning left

Turning right

To turn left, squeeze your left hand on the rein and pull it back a little way. Let your other hand go forward as the pony turns its head.

Pull your right hand back to turn right. Try to sit straight. When you turn, keep your pony moving steadily by squeezing with both heels.

Practicing your skills

Your instructor may put out a circle of cones in the ring to help you practice turning. You could also ride your pony in and out of a line of plastic pots or try riding around poles.

Remember to look ahead to where you want to go.

Secret steps

Draw two lines. A friend stands behind one and turns his back on the riders, who line up behind the other.

Draw the lines about 16 yards (15 meters) apart.

The friend counts aloud to ten and the riders walk up to him. On "ten" he turns around and everyone stops. Anyone still moving goes back to their line. The friend turns away and counts again. The first rider to reach him wins.

When you turn, keep the pony moving steadily by squeezing with both heels.

Make the turns as smooth as you can.

Trotting

When a pony trots, it moves its legs two at a time. This makes trotting feel much bumpier than walking.

See if you can move up and down with your arms folded.

Knot your reins to keep them out of the way.

At first when you trot, someone leads you so that you can just sit still, holding the saddle. This is a sitting trot. Try to count "one-two" in time with the bumps.

Trotting is easier if you rise up and down. When you are used to your pony trotting, practice rising while your pony is standing still.

To rise, lean forward slightly and push into the stirrups to lift your bottom out of the saddle. When you sit down again, land as gently as you can.

Rising trot

Use the neckstrap to help you.

Don't rise too high.

Be careful not to pull on the reins.

To try rising while the pony is trotting, count "one-two" again in time with the bumps. Rise on "one".

Sit when you say "two" but get ready to rise again as soon as your bottom is in the saddle.

When you can rise up and down steadily, you can hold the reins so you can steer the pony.

Going from a walk to a trot

When you trot, you need shorter reins because the pony holds its head higher. Shorten them just before you start to trot.

Then squeeze the pony's sides with both heels and say "trot." Sit for the first few bumps, then begin to rise.

To go back to walking, briefly close your legs on the pony and say "wa-alk". Tighten and loosen the reins until the pony obeys.

Tip

If the sitting trot is very bumpy, hold onto the front of the saddle with one hand, to keep your bottom still in the saddle.

Trotting maze

To practice steering, ask your instructor to place plastic pots in pairs like this. Then see if you can make your pony trot between each pair. Go back to the beginning if you miss any.

Use your legs to keep the pony going while you guide it with your reins.

Try not to go too fast.

How to get off a pony

Here you can find out how to get off and lead a pony safely. Getting off a pony is called dismounting. Make the pony stand still before you begin.

Practice mounting and dismounting from both sides.

Dismounting

Give your leg a good swing up when you lean forward.

Keep your leg straight or it may get caught on the saddle.

1. Take both feet out of the stirrups. Then hold the reins in your left hand and rest it on the pony's neck, as in the second picture.

2. Put your right hand on the front of the saddle. Now lean forward and swing your right leg over the saddle.

3. Keep your left hand on the reins as you land on the ground. Be careful not to hit the pony with your right leg as you dismount.

Running up the stirrups

Slide the stirrup up the side of the leather loop which touches the saddle.

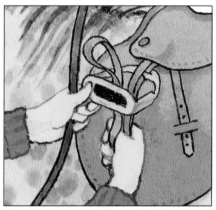

Remember to keep hold of the reins the whole time.

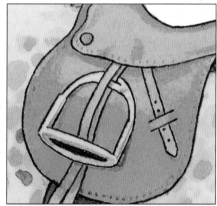

Stirrups must be run up or they will bang against the pony's side.

Always run up the stirrups before leading your pony away. Still holding the reins, slide the stirrup to the top of the leather loop.

Then take the stirrup in your left hand with the reins, and pull the loop back through the stirrup with your right hand.

When you have finished, your stirrups should look like this. Try playing 'Musical sacks' to practice running up the stirrups.

14

Leading a pony

Stand on the pony's left side and pull the reins over its head. This makes it easier to lead the pony.

With your right hand, hold both reins close to the pony's mouth. Pick up the ends with your left hand so you do not trip over them.

Say "walk" to the pony. Begin to walk and the pony should walk beside you. Say "ha-aalt" calmly and stand still when you want it to stop.

Stay beside the pony's shoulder.

Some instructors may tell you to hold the reins with your little finger nearest to the bit.

Tip	You must never wind the reins around your hand as you cannot let go quickly if you need to.

Musical sacks

The players must run up their stirrups before leading their ponies.

You can play 'Musical sacks' with friends and your instructor or a helper. You will need a radio and some sacks. The helper puts down a sack for each player except one. The players ride around while the helper plays the music.

When the helper stops the music, everyone gets off and leads their pony to a sack. The rider who doesn't get to one is out. The helper takes a sack away and restarts the music. The rest ride around. The game goes on until one rider is left.

Better riding

It takes a lot of practice to become a good rider and make your pony do what you want it to. Working on exercises in a ring helps you learn to have full control of your pony.

Ring movements

The instructor uses special commands to tell you what to do. "Go large" means go around the ring. If you go to the left, you are "on the left rein".

If you go to the right, you are "on the right rein". On "change the rein", everyone turns across the ring, one behind the other and goes the other way.

When you are on the left rein, all your turns will be to the left.

Turning in

For "turn in and halt", everyone turns their pony off the track. Then they stop and stand in a line.

Using a riding crop

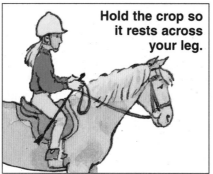

Hold the crop so it rests across your leg.

When you can ride well, you can carry a crop. Only use it if your pony ignores your leg signals.

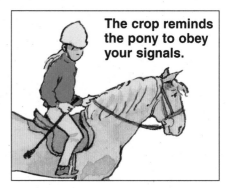

The crop reminds the pony to obey your signals.

Take the reins in one hand. With the other hand hit the pony once with the crop, just behind your leg.

Things to remember

This is a safe distance between ponies.

This is too close.

When you are turning, push with the leg on the inside of the bend.

If you are keeping a safe distance, you will be able to see the bottom of the tail of the pony in front, through your pony's ears.

Sit quietly, keeping your head, hips and heels in a straight line. Use the signals you have learned to keep the pony moving steadily.

Steer carefully around the corners of the ring. You can stop your pony cutting a corner by pushing its side with your leg.

Always keep a safe distance from the pony in front of you. Remember, the pony in front might kick out if you ride too close.

Look out for letters

There are usually letters marked around the ring in this order. If the instructor tells you to do something at a letter, give signals to your pony in plenty of time.

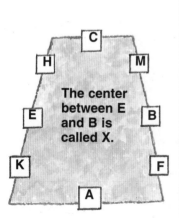

The center between E and B is called X.

Try to get your pony to obey just as your shoulders are level with the letter.

Riding clothes

Here are some clothes you might like to buy, if you ride a lot. Everyday ones wear out quickly. You can often buy clothes like these second-hand from a riding school.

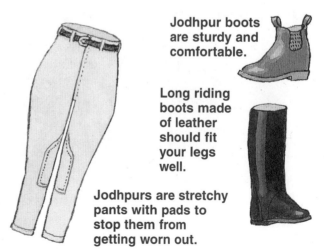

Jodhpur boots are sturdy and comfortable.

Long riding boots made of leather should fit your legs well.

Jodhpurs are stretchy pants with pads to stop them from getting worn out.

Cantering

When you are good at steering your pony in a trot, you can learn to canter. Cantering is faster than trotting but it feels much smoother.

Asking your pony to canter

1. Begin a canter at a corner of the ring. Make your pony trot steadily up to the corner.

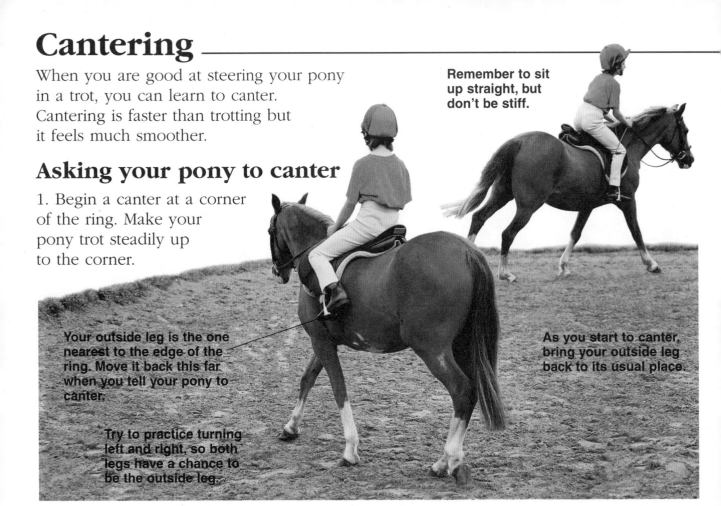

Remember to sit up straight, but don't be stiff.

Your outside leg is the one nearest to the edge of the ring. Move it back this far when you tell your pony to canter.

Try to practice turning left and right, so both legs have a chance to be the outside leg.

As you start to canter, bring your outside leg back to its usual place.

2. Stop rising as you begin to turn. Move your outside leg back and squeeze it against the pony's side.

3. As you squeeze the pony, say "canter" firmly. The pony seems to rock back and forth as it canters.

4. Sit up and let your hands move so that you do not pull against the pony. Try to keep sitting tall.

How the pony moves

The leading leg is in front of the others when it is on the ground.

When a pony canters, the hoof beats come in sets of three. First the pony puts down one back leg.

Then the pony puts down its other back leg together with a front leg on the opposite side.

Lastly, the pony puts down its other front leg. This is the leading leg. It is always the last one to come down.

Trotting again

It is easiest to get your pony to trot along a straight side of the ring.

To ask your pony to trot, first shorten your reins (see page 10). This helps the pony feel your commands on the reins through its mouth. Then close your legs firmly, squeeze and say "tro-ot."

Swinging your legs

Hold your reins in one hand.

Practice moving one leg by itself while the pony is walking. Take your feet out of the stirrups, lift up each stirrup and cross the leathers in front of the saddle. Now, swing one leg backward and forward from the knee. Try to keep the other leg still.

Staying steady

If you stay calm and relaxed, your pony will canter much more easily.

You might feel yourself tipping forward. Holding the saddle will help you stay upright.

At first, just canter a few steps at a time until you get used to it. To begin with, put your reins in your outside hand and hold the front of the saddle with your other hand.

Disobedient ponies

Sometimes a pony may just trot faster when you ask it to canter. If this happens, slow back down to a steady trot along a straight side of the ring. Then ask it to canter again at the next corner.

Your pony may canter more easily if you ask it to canter just as it goes over a pole.

Your instructor will put a pole across the corner.

19

Jumping

When a pony jumps, you can feel it stretch out its neck and spring up and forward. It is easier to keep your balance if you bend forward as the pony jumps. This is called the jumping position.

Practicing the position

You can practice the jumping position while your pony is standing still. Keeping your back straight, bend forward from your hips. This is called folding (see below). Push your heels down at the same time. If this seems difficult, shorten your stirrups by one or two holes and try again.

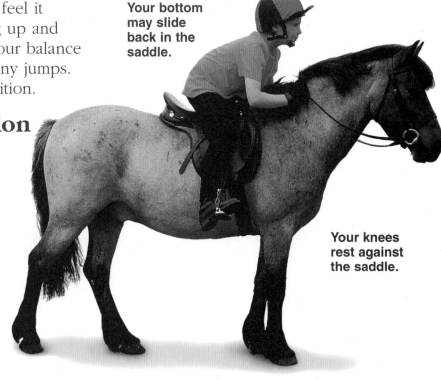

Your bottom may slide back in the saddle.

Your knees rest against the saddle.

Folding

Keep your back straight.

Bend from the hips, not your waist.

When you go into the jumping position, try to fold forward from your hips. This makes sure you are far enough forward to keep your balance as the pony jumps. Try folding without your pony at first.

Going over poles

Steer straight for the middle of each pole.

Stay in the jumping position as you go over them all.

To practice the position while the pony is moving, walk or trot over poles. As your pony steps over a pole, it stretches out its neck. Push your hands toward its mouth so the reins don't pull the pony back.

Riding up to a jump

Ride straight for the middle of the jump.

When you are good at going over poles, you can trot your pony over a small jump. Trot steadily up to the jump.

Fold forward at your hips but keep your bottom in the saddle as you go up to the jump. Look ahead, not down at the jump.

Show jumping

The poles fall down easily if they are touched.

Show jumpers ride over a course of colored jumps. They try to jump over all of the fences the first time, without knocking any down.

Going over a jump

As your pony leaves the ground, your bottom may come out of the saddle.

Keep your back flat.

Your hands should reach a long way down the pony's neck.

Keep your heels down.

1. Hold your legs firm against the pony. Fold forward as it takes off, pushing down with your heels to keep your balance.

2. Keep looking straight ahead, but let your hands go forward as the pony stretches out its neck over the jump.

3. As the pony touches the ground and you land in the saddle, begin to sit up. Get ready to steer the pony where you want to go next.

Games and outings

As you become a better and more experienced rider, you can have fun doing different things with your pony.

Riding outside

Riding in the open is called hacking. At first an experienced rider can lead you from their horse to help you to control your pony. If you go on a road, keep in to the side so that cars can pass you. It is safer and more fun to ride along tracks and fields instead. Your instructor may take you for a hack during a lesson.

Greedy ponies

Grass reins

Sometimes your pony may stop to eat grass. Make it walk by squeezing hard with both legs. Use one rein to pull up its head if you need to.

If this doesn't work, extra straps, called grass reins, can be used. They go from the bridle to the saddle and stop your pony from putting its head down to graze.

Giving treats

Keep your hand flat as you hold out the treat.

You might like to reward your pony with an apple or carrot after your ride, but always ask your instructor first. Slice carrots lengthwise so your pony doesn't choke.

Gymkhanas

Horse shows sometimes have games competitions for ponies called gymkhanas. You might like to join the Pony Club which organizes games for its members. For details of the Pony Club see page 32.

One game you might play is the sack race. Carrying a sack, you ride your pony to the center line. Then you quickly dismount and get into your sack. You must then jump along beside your pony.

You can cross the stirrups over the saddle to stop them from flapping around.

Bending races

Each pony goes along its own line of poles.

In this game, you steer your pony in and out of a line of poles. Then you go around the last pole, racing in and out again, back to the start.

Flag races

There is a set of flags and a tub for each person.

Starting by a tub, you race to a set of flags. Then pick up one flag at a time and race back to your tub to drop it in.

Ribbons

If you are lucky and are first, second or third, you may win a ribbon. Even if you are last, remember to pat your pony for trying.

In the barn

Most ponies live in a barn for part of the day. The rest of the time they go out in a field so they can eat the grass.

However new a rider you are, you can help out at your stables.

A pony's barn

Some barns have long rows of compartments called stalls. A pony can be tied up in each one. This takes up less room and the ponies have company.

Other barns are like small rooms. The pony can be let loose inside them and can move around or lie down easily. Doors open halfway, so the pony can look out.

Straw makes the ground comfortable to stand on. Dirty straw and droppings are taken away every day in a wheelbarrow. This is called mucking out.

What a pony eats

Ponies eat other food besides grass. Here are some things they can eat or drink.

Ponies need clean water near them all the time.

Pony treats are made of chopped up grass and cereals.

Hay is dried grass. It's put in a net for traveling, and in a feeder or on the ground in a pony's stall.

Oats are like breakfast oats but with the husks still on.

Bran comes from wheat.

Ponies can become sick if they eat too much, so never give your pony any food unless you have asked an adult first.

Catching a pony

When you want to lead a pony out of a field, you need to use a halter like this one. Carry it into the field and fasten the noseband before you go near the pony.

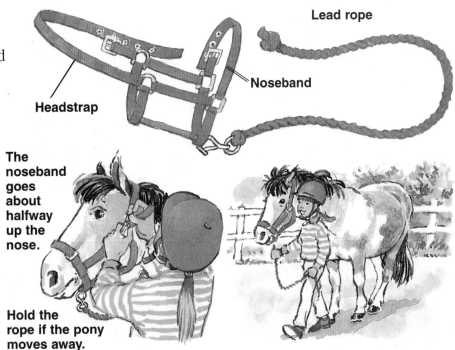

Lead rope

Headstrap

Noseband

Ask an adult to help you at first.

The noseband goes about halfway up the nose.

Hold the rope if the pony moves away.

1. Call the pony's name and walk calmly up to its shoulder. Place the lead rope over the pony's neck.

2. Slip the noseband over the pony's nose. Then fasten the headstrap just behind the pony's ears.

3. Now take the rope off the pony's neck. Holding the rope, say "walk" and lead it to the barn.

Tying a pony up

Most barns have metal rings on the wall. Tie your pony up to the lead rope loops attached to the rings.

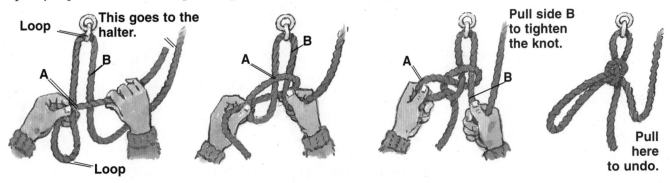

Loop

This goes to the halter.

B

A

Loop

B

A

Pull side B to tighten the knot.

A

B

Pull here to undo.

Push your pony's lead rope through the loop. Make a loop in the lead rope and take side A over B.

Bring A behind the first loop. Make a loop with the end of A and pull through the first loop (third picture).

To undo the knot, pull hard on the free end of the rope. Always use a knot like this that you can undo quickly.

Grooming

Ponies need to be brushed to keep them clean. This is called grooming. Before you begin, tie your pony up so it stands still.

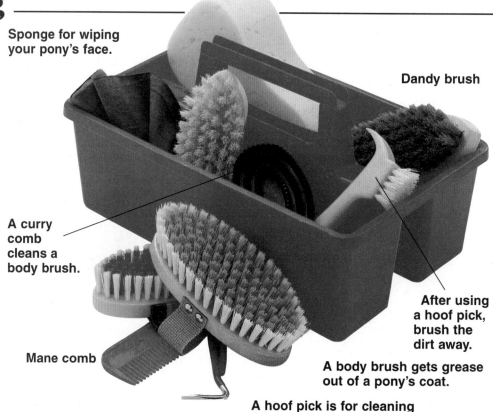

Sponge for wiping your pony's face.

Dandy brush

A curry comb cleans a body brush.

Mane comb

After using a hoof pick, brush the dirt away.

A body brush gets grease out of a pony's coat.

A hoof pick is for cleaning out a pony's feet.

What to use

Here are some of the things you need to groom a pony. When you use them for the first time, ask your instructor to show you what to do. You can carry everything in a tack box like this.

Using a hoof pick

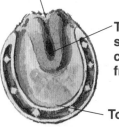

Heel

Most of the inside of a hoof is hard horn.

This is a soft part called the frog.

Toe

Ponies wear metal shoes to stop their hooves from getting worn down.

Run your hand down from the very top of each leg.

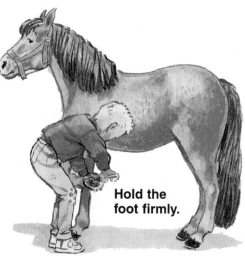

Hold the foot firmly.

A pony's foot, or hoof, is hollow so dirt gets trapped inside. The picture above shows the underneath part of the hoof.

To clean inside the hooves, ask your pony to lift each foot in turn, by running your hand down its leg and saying "up".

Run the hoof pick from the heel to the toe, beside the frog, to get the dirt out. Be very careful not to dig the hook into the frog.

Brushing a pony

Groom your pony as soon as its coat is dry after your ride.

Sweep the brush backward and forward.

Push the curry comb away from you, like this.

Look for cuts in your pony's skin. Tell an adult if you find any. Rub off mud and dried sweat with a dandy brush. It's scratchy, so don't use it on the pony's head.

Use the body brush in long, firm strokes all over the pony's body. Lean on it slightly so it pushes through the coat. Brush in the same direction as the hairs grow.

As you brush, hold the curry comb ready in your other hand. Every so often, clean the oil and dust from the body brush by rubbing the curry comb against it.

Be very careful not to hurt your pony's eyes or nostrils.

Stand to one side while you brush out the tail.

Waterproof coats

Don't worry about pulling on your pony's mane or tail. Ponies enjoy it.

Ponies who live outside groom each other using their lips and teeth.

Put down the curry comb and hold the pony's nose with your free hand. This keeps its head still while you brush it.

Brush the mane and tail with the body brush, a few hairs at a time. If it is very tangled, pull it apart gently with your hands first.

Many ponies live outside at night. Natural oils in their coat help them to stay warm and dry. These ponies are only groomed lightly so as not to brush out too much oil.

27

Tacking up

Putting on a saddle and bridle is called tacking up. It takes practice so ask someone to help you while you learn.

A well-fitting saddle shouldn't touch the pony's backbone or pinch its shoulders. Tie your pony up before you put one on.

Putting on a saddle

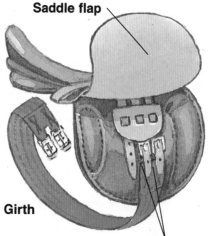

Saddle flap

Girth

Use the front two straps.

1. Lift the flap on the right side of the saddle. Make sure that one end of the girth is buckled to the straps under the flap.

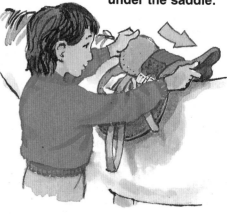

Slide the saddle back so that the hairs lie flat under the saddle.

Both stirrups should be run up (see page 14).

2. Lay the girth over the saddle and go to the pony's left side. Lift the saddle onto the pony's shoulders and slide it into place.

Never walk around behind your pony. Duck under the rope to change sides.

3. Go around the front of the pony and pull the girth back over the saddle, so it hangs down. Then go back to the left-hand side.

Use the front straps again.

4. Now pick up the end of the girth and bring it under the pony's tummy. Buckle it onto the straps under the left saddle flap.

Keep your hand flat.

5. Remember to run your hand under the girth to make sure that it is not pinching the pony's skin. Check this on both sides.

Putting on the bridle

Reins

Throatlatch

Noseband

Bit

Undo this buckle on the halter.

Keep your fingers outside the pony's mouth.

1. Make sure that the buckles on the noseband and the throatlatch are undone. Everything else stays as it is.

2. Go to the pony's left side. Put the reins over the pony's head so they rest on its neck. Then undo the halter and slip it off.

3. Rest the bit on your left hand. Open the pony's mouth by pressing the corner with your thumb, then slip the bit inside.

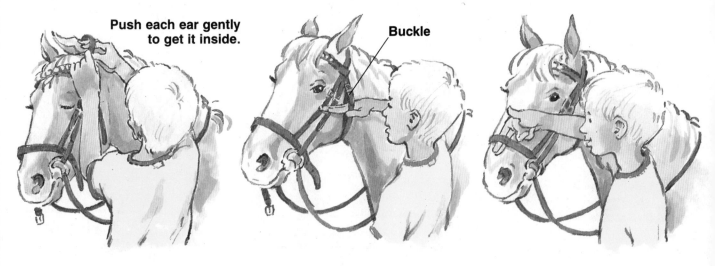

Push each ear gently to get it inside.

Buckle

4. Put the top of the bridle over the pony's ears. Smooth out any pieces of mane that get trapped under the bridle.

5. Fasten the buckle on the throatlatch. The throatlatch fits fairly loosely. You should be able to get your hand inside like this.

6. Finally, fasten the buckle on the noseband. The noseband should be just loose enough for you to get two fingers inside.

Untacking

Taking off the saddle and bridle is called untacking. Lead the pony into its stall before you untack it. You also need to have its halter with you.

Once you have led your pony into the barn, remember to take the reins back over its neck. Never leave them to dangle.

Taking off the bridle

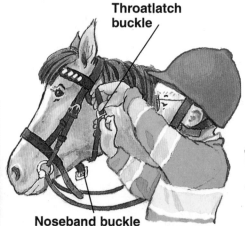

Throatlatch buckle

Noseband buckle

1. Undo the buckle on the noseband, just above the pony's chin. Then undo the buckle on the throatlatch. This buckle is always on the pony's left side.

2. Lift the top of the bridle and gently pull it up and over the pony's ears. Rest your left hand on the pony's nose to stop it from raising its head.

Do not let the bit bang the pony's teeth. This hurts a lot.

Hold the pony by the reins if it tries to walk off.

Loop the reins on your shoulder while you tie up the pony.

3. Put your right hand under the pony's chin. Bring it up to hold the bridle and gently slide the bit out of the pony's mouth.

4. Rest the bridle on your shoulder while you are putting on and fastening the pony's halter (see page 25).

5. Take the reins over the pony's head, lifting them high over its ears. Put the bridle in a safe place while you take off the saddle.

Taking off the saddle

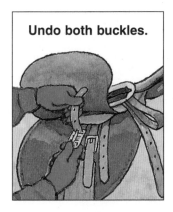

Undo both buckles.

1. Start on the pony's left side. Lift up the saddle flap and hold it up while you undo the buckles on the girth.

2. Keep hold of the girth. If it falls it may bang the pony's leg. Lower it carefully so that it hangs without swinging.

3. Go around the front of the pony. Pick up the girth on the other side and loop it over the saddle.

4. Put one hand on the front of the saddle and one on the back. Carefully slide the saddle off the pony.

Putting tack away

When you have finished untacking your pony, you should put the saddle and bridle away. All tack is kept in a tack room.

Saddles go onto long saddle racks. Bridles are hung on hooks.

You should carry the bridle over one shoulder, like a bag. To carry the saddle, pick it up with both hands underneath and rest it against your chest.

A tack room is full of riding equipment.

Cleaning and polishing tack helps to keep it in good condition.

If you need to put the saddle down for a moment, before putting it away, stand it on its front like this.

Index

Thanks to:-

Ben and Daniel Edmed, Philippa Howe, Madelaine Kasch, Holly Samuel, Annabel and Camilla Swift; Gaynor Osborne, Teresa Watson and the Bradbourne Riding and Training Centre, Sevenoaks; Chloe Albert and riders and ponies at the Trent Park Equestrian Centre; Hannah Paul and Ian McNee; Susan Hightower for help with the American edition.

ISBN 0-590-63161-6

Useful addresses

U.S. Pony Clubs, Inc.
4071 IronWorks Pike
Lexington, KY 40511-8462

American Horse Show Association
Suite 409
220 East 42nd St.
New York, NY 10017

Equestrian Federation of Australia Inc.
52 Kensington Road
Rose Park
S. Australia 5067

Canadian Equestrian Federation
1600 James Naismith Drive
Gloucester
Ontario
K1B 5N4
Canada

New Zealand Equestrian Federation
PO Box 6146
Te Aro
Wellington
New Zealand